D0874135

MAY 2007

CB

Amazon River Dolphins

By Sandra Donovan

Steadwell Books

Raintree Steck-Vaughn Publishers

A Harcourt Company

Austin · New York

www.raintreesteckvaughn.com

ANIMALS OF THE RAIN FOREST

Published by Raintree Steck-Vaughn Publishers, an imprint of Steck-Vaughn Company.

Library of Congress Cataloging-in-Publication Data
Donovan, Sandra.
    Amazon river dolphins / Sandra Donovan.
     p. cm.—(Animals of the rain forest)
    Includes bibliographical references (p.).
    Summary: Introduces the unusual dolphins that have adapted to life in the Amazon River Region of South America, explores their habitats, and explains why they are endangered and what we can do to protect them.
    ISBN 0-7398-5367-8
    1. Boto—Juvenile literature. 4. Tucuxi—Juvenile literature. [1. River dolphins. 2. Dolphins. 3. Endangered species. 4. Amazon River Region.] I. Title. II. Series.

    QL737.C436 D66 2002
    599.53'8'09811—dc21   2001048974

Printed and bound in the United States of America
1 2 3 4 5 6 7 8 9 10 WZ 05 04 03 02

Produced by Compass Books

Photo Acknowledgments
Corbis/APF, 11; Thomas Henningsen, 8, 26, 28–29; Tamara McGuire, title page, 6, 24; Minden Pictures, 22; Flip Nicklin, cover, 12, 14, 18.

Editor: Bryon Cahill
Consultant: Sean Dolan

Content Consultant
Tamara McGuire
River Dolphin Research Project
Pacaya-Samiria National Reserve, Peru

This book supports the National Science Standards.

Contents

MEXICO

BELIZE
HONDURAS

GUATEMALA
EL SALVADOR
NICARAGUA

Caribbean
Sea

COSTA RICA

PANAMA

ECUADOR

COLOMBIA

VENEZUELA

North
Atlantic
Ocean

GUYANA
SURINAME

FRENCH
GUIANA
(FRANCE)

ORINOCO
RIVER

AMAZON
RIVER

PERU

BRAZIL

BOLIVIA

South
Pacific
Ocean

CHILE

PARAGUAY

South
Atlantic
Ocean

ARGENTINA

URUGUAY

Range of the
Amazon River
Dolphins

Surrounding
Land

Water

Borders

Rivers

N
W E
S

4

A Quick Look at Amazon River Dolphins

What do Amazon River dolphins look like?

Amazon River dolphins have long, smooth bodies. They have fins and tails to help them swim. They can be different colors, such as pink or gray.

Where do Amazon River dolphins live?

Amazon River dolphins live in the rivers of the Amazon area in South America. Some dolphins can also live in the Atlantic Ocean off the coast of South and Central America.

What do Amazon River dolphins eat?

Amazon River dolphins eat mainly fish. They may sometimes eat crabs or other small animals that live in rivers.

This Amazon River dolphin belongs to the Platanistidae family.

Amazon River Dolphins in the Rain Forest

A mazon River dolphins are one of the few kinds of mammals that live in water. A mammal is a warm-blooded animal with a backbone. Female mammals give birth to live young and feed them with milk from their bodies. Warm-blooded animals have a body temperature that stays the same, no matter what the temperature is outside. Most mammals have fur that keeps them warm. Instead of fur, dolphins have a thick layer of fat called **blubber**.

Most river dolphins of the Amazon belong to the dolphin family called *Platanistidae* (PLA-tan-is-ti-day). The other river dolphins belong to the family Delphinidae. Platanistidae are dolphins that live in warm rivers. Most other dolphins live in the ocean.

This dolphin has swum to the surface to breathe through its blowhole.

Where Do River Dolphins Live?

Only a few rivers in the world have dolphins living in them. Amazon River dolphins live mainly in South America's Amazon and Orinoco (ohr-in-OH-koh) Rivers.

Rivers are freshwater bodies of water. This means that the water has very little or no salt in it. Oceans are saltwater. Most Amazon River dolphins live only in freshwater. Some also live in parts of the Atlantic Ocean off the coast of South and Central America.

Amazon River dolphins have **adapted** to live in rivers. To adapt means to change in order to better fit an environment. Dolphins have one **flipper** on each side of their body to use for swimming. Their tails have wide parts called **flukes** on the end. Dolphins move their tails and flukes up and down to help push them through water. In order to breathe, dolphins have **blowholes.** They go up to the surface of the water and breathe in the outside air. They have to do this every three minutes.

River dolphins live in most parts of the river, except near waterfalls and estuaries. Estuaries are places where river water flows into ocean water. Dolphins also do not live in rapids, or fast-flowing water. It is hard to swim in these places. When there is little rain, the water level of rivers becomes very shallow. Shallow water can prevent dolphins from getting to certain parts of the rivers. People also build dams to block the flow of river water. Dams stop dolphins, too.

Kinds of Amazon River Dolphins

The two **species** of river dolphins that live in the Amazon are the boto (BOH-toh) and the tucuxi (too-KOO-shee). A species is a group of animals or plants closely related to each other.

Botos have a wide freshwater range in the Amazon. They are also called pink dolphins because some of them have a pinkish color. Some people call them bufeo colorados (boo-FEE-oh col-oh-RAH-dohs). Bufeo sounds like the puffing, grunting noise they make when they spray air and water out of their blowholes. At the water's surface, the dolphin blows away any water that has pooled in its blowhole before it breathes.

Tucuxi can live in saltwater as well as rivers. Sometimes people call them bufeo gris (boo-FEE-oh GREE) because of the sound they make when breathing. Gris means gray, which is the color of these dolphins.

Botos and tucuxis are both dolphins. But they have differences, too. Botos have lumpy heads with longer, heavier bodies. They can weigh almost twice as much as tucuxis.

Botos can swim better than tucuxis in shallow water and around objects. Botos have a special

 This is a pink-colored boto dolphin.

neck. Their neck bones are not fused, or joined together. Because of this, the boto can turn and move its neck. This makes it easier to swim around objects. Like other dolphins, the tucuxi's bones are fused. It cannot turn its head and neck as far.

The boto can also use its flippers in special ways. It can paddle forward with one flipper, and paddle backward with the other flipper. This lets the boto swim in all directions.

 You can see the long beak-like snout on this boto dolphin.

What Do Amazon River Dolphins Look Like?

Amazon River dolphins are between 4 feet (1.2 m) and 8 feet (2.4 m) long. Botos are the largest river dolphins, and they grow up to 8 feet (2.4 m). They weigh from 400 to 540 pounds (150 to 200 kg). Tucuxis are smaller, ranging from about 4 feet (1.3 m) to just more than 5 feet (1.6 m). They weigh up to 135 pounds (50 kg).

Tucuxi are gray with light gray bands on their sides. Their undersides are sometime light pink if they are active. Botos' coloring ranges from gray to bright pink. The pink color comes from blood flowing close to the surface of its skin. Scientists are not sure why some botos are gray and others are pink. They think age or readiness to mate may change the coloring. When botos become excited or more active, they sometimes change color from gray to pink.

Botos have a large head with a long beak. They have about 100 teeth in their mouth. They look like they are always smiling. Tucuxis have a smaller, rounder head with a shorter beak. They have about 140 teeth.

Both kinds of dolphin use flippers and fins to help them change direction while they swim. Botos have two pectoral (pek-TOHR-al) fins on their underside. They have a long, low ridge that runs down their back to their tail. Tucuxis also have two pectoral fins. But, like sharks and most other dolphins, they have a triangle-shaped dorsal (DOHR-sal) fin that sticks up on their lower back.

You can see the cone-shaped teeth of this boto dolphin.

What Amazon River Dolphins Eat

Most Amazon River dolphins are **piscivorous**. This means they eat mainly fish. They also may eat other animals that live in the rivers, including crabs.

Dolphins have special cone-shaped teeth. This shape helps them grab onto and hold slippery fish. Boto dolphins eat more than 50 species of fish. Tucuxis eat about 30 species of fish. There are only about 15 species that both botos and tucuxis eat, even though they live in the same areas.

Tucuxis are smaller than botos, but they eat up to two times more. This is because they need more energy than botos do. Tucuxis swim faster and are more active than botos.

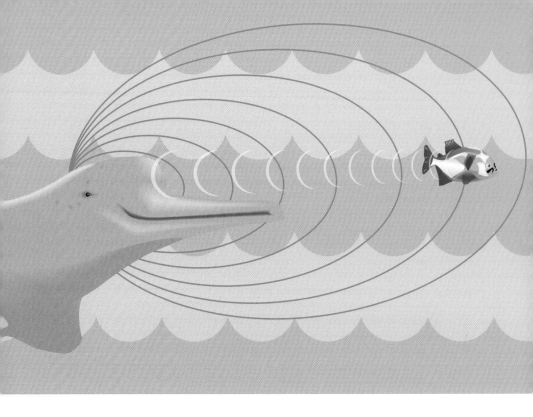

▲ This illustration shows how dolphins use echolocation to find food.

Finding Food

Amazon River dolphins have two main ways of finding food. Boto dolphins have small hairs on their noses. They use this hair to feel for food in the mud at the bottom of the river. They are the only kind of adult dolphin that has any hair on their body. Both kinds of river dolphins dig in the mud with their beaks. This is how they find crabs and other animals that live in the mud.

One of their favorite foods is the catfish. They stick their beaks in the muddy riverbanks to find the places these fish are hiding. Then, they catch the fish by grabbing them with their beak. They use their teeth to catch and hold the fish.

Like other dolphins, river dolphins usually find food by using **echolocation**. This means that they use echoes to find food and other objects in the water.

To use echolocation, a dolphin sends out a sound. The sound travels ahead of the dolphin. It moves through the water until it hits an object. Then, it bounces back to the dolphin. From this echo, the dolphin can tell how far away an object is. It can also tell how big the object is. This helps them find food in dark water of the river.

Sometimes Amazon River dolphins swim upside down. Scientists believe that echolocation may work better this way.

Boto dolphins have an unusually large, fatty bump on their heads called an oily melon. Scientists think that the oily melon is used for echolocation.

These two botos may be living together as a group.

An Amazon River Dolphin's Life Cycle

River dolphins live in large or small groups. They may mate with another dolphin in their group, or they may mate with a dolphin from another group.

Scientists do not know a lot about how river dolphins mate. They think the season of birth depends on the species of dolphin and where it lives. The dolphins seem to give birth during different seasons in some parts of their range and year-round in others. Females produce young about once every two to three years. Ten to twelve months after mating, a female dolphin gives birth to a baby dolphin.

Young dolphins are called calves. They are usually born tail first.

Calves

Calves are very large at birth. They can be almost half the size of their mothers. Newborn botos are usually about 2.3 to 2.6 feet (70 to 80 cm) long. Tucuxi calves can weigh up to 20 pounds (75 kg) at birth.

Newborn calves know how to swim and move about on their own as soon as they are born. They can also see and hear very well at birth.

Calves are bluish gray or dark gray. This color helps camouflage them. Camouflage is coloring or patterns that help an animal blend in with its surroundings. The color helps young calves blend in with the dark water while they are swimming.

Calves receive food and protection from their mothers. Like other mammals, female dolphins feed their young milk from their bodies. This is called nursing. Calves nurse until they are one to two years old.

Calves grow very quickly. They can eat some kinds of fish by the time they are six months old. By the time they are two years old, they stop nursing. Calves stay with their mothers for up to three years. They learn how to fish and find their

This mother dolphin is teaching her calf how to move around the river.

way around their river homes. When they are five years old, they begin mating.

Scientists think river dolphins continue to grow throughout their lives. Scientists think that boto dolphins live between 15 and 25 years. They do not know how long tucuxi dolphins live.

▲ This tucuxi dolphin is swimming on
its side.

A Day in the Life of a River Dolphin

Amazon River dolphins are social animals.
They like to touch each other with their beaks
and their flippers. Scientists have seen river
dolphins in groups of two to five. The tucuxi may
be in bigger groups of as many as 50 dolphins.
Scientists do not know if these dolphins always
live together in groups or if they gather in

groups only for a short time to hunt for fish.

River dolphins use sound to communicate with other dolphins. Communicate means to send and receive messages. The dolphins make whistles and clicks underwater. Other dolphins understand what these sounds mean.

Amazon River dolphins spend most of their day swimming in the rivers. They can swim up to 12 miles (30 km) each day. Boto dolphins swim very slowly. They do not jump out of the water very often. Tucuxi dolphins are very fast swimmers.

River dolphins may slap their flukes on the water's surface. They jump out of the water. Sometimes they raise their heads above the water and push their bodies forward by moving their tails. This is called spy-hopping. At times, they swim behind or along the side of boats.

During the rainy season, the water level rises, and the rivers overflow into the surrounding forests. Then, the river dolphins swim among the trees. Botos can move between the trees better than tucuxis because they can turn their necks. In the dry season, the water level is much lower. The forest dries up, and the river dolphins return to the main rivers.

Scientists do not know how many boto dolphins are alive in the wild.

The Future of
Amazon River Dolphins

Most dolphins are friendly to people. In South America, some people say that the tucuxi bring good news.

Scientists are not sure how many Amazon River dolphins are living, but they know that they are in danger. The dolphins have few natural predators. A predator is an animal that hunts another for food. People are the biggest threat to the dolphins.

More and more people are moving into the rain forests of South America. This causes trouble for the dolphins. People cut down trees around the rivers. This means that there is less food for smaller fish. These smaller fish die without food. In turn, there is less food for river dolphins.

These scientists are studying this dolphin. They will release it back into the river.

What Will Happen to River Dolphins?

Fishermen sometimes kill dolphins because they believe the dolphins are pests. The dolphins sometimes bite holes in the fishermen's nets and eat the fish.

Fishermen also accidentally catch dolphins in their nets. Sometimes dolphins can tear

Dolphins cannot fall into a deep sleep because they must remember to breathe. If they slept, they would stop breathing and drown. Instead, dolphins rest with one side of their brain awake, so they will remember to breathe.

themselves free of these nets. But usually, they drown because they cannot get free.

Pollution is also a problem in the Amazon and Orinoco Rivers. Waste from large cities sometimes flows into the rivers, which then **pollutes** them. Also, people looking for gold and oil around the rain forests pollute the rivers. Pollution makes the river dolphins sick and can even kill them.

People are going to have to work hard to save Amazon River dolphins. Some countries already have laws against killing dolphins. Other countries have laws against polluting the rivers. More work is needed to make sure the Amazon River dolphins will survive in their rain forest homes.

blowhole
see page 9

beak
see page 13

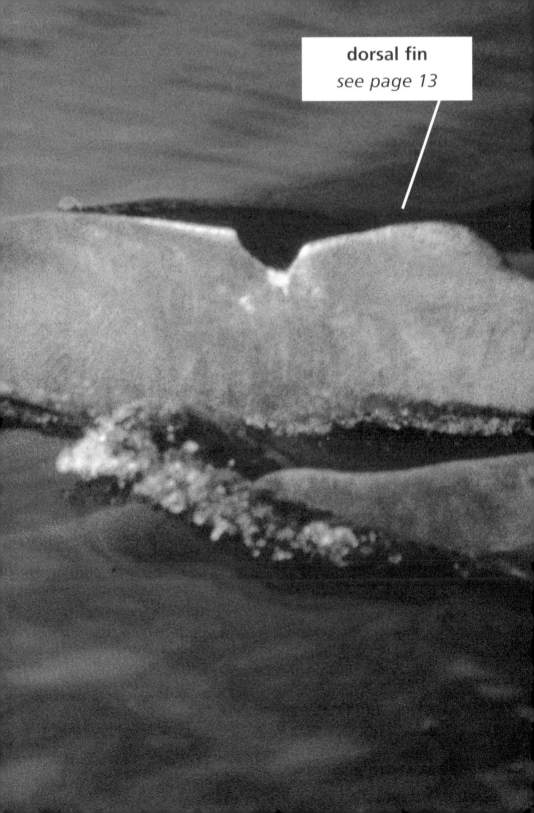

dorsal fin
see page 13

Glossary

adapted (uh-DAP-ted)—changed in order to better fit an environment

blowholes (BLOH-HOHLS)—openings used for breathing

blubber (BLUH-ber)—a thick layer of fat that keeps animals warm

echolocation (EK-oh-loh-KAY-shun)—when animals use echoes to locate food and other objects in the water

flipper (FLIP-ur)—a body part on a dolphin's side that helps it change direction as it swims

flukes (FLEWKS)—the wide parts at the end of a dolphin's tail

pesticide (PESS-tuh-side)—chemicals made by people used to kill pests, such as insects

piscivorous (puh-SI-vuh-ruhs)—animals that eat mainly fish

pollutes (puh-LOOTS)—to make an area dirty with garbage or other things made by people

species (SPEE-sees)—a group of animals or plants most closely related to each other in the scientific classification system

Internet Sites

International Dolphin Watch
www.idw.org

Virtual Explorers
www.virtualexplorers.org

Useful Address

Dolphin Research Center
P.O. Box 522875
Marathon Shores, FL 33052

Books to Read

Montgomery, Sy. *Encantado: Pink Dolphin of the Amazon.* Boston: Houghton Mifflin, 2002.

Perry, Phyllis Jean. *Freshwater Giants: Hippopotamus, River Dolphins, and Manatees.* New York: Franklin Watts, 1999.

Index